WHAT SLOWS OUR SPIRITUAL PROGRESS?

Reference Notes

This pamphlet contains the transcript of
Recording #295-B, a Joel Goldsmith class
from the 1959 Chicago Open Class: Tape 1, side 2.
This recording is currently available in audiotape,
CD, or MP3 format at www.joelgoldsmith.com.

Other Titles in This Series

Supply
Metaphysical Healing
Meditation and Prayer
Business and Salesmanship
Ye Are the Light
The Real Teacher and The Seven Steps
Truth
The Secret of the Twenty-Third Psalm
Love and Gratitude
I Am the Vine
The Deep Silence of My Peace
The Fourth Dimension of Life
Contemplative Meditation with Scripture
The Easter of Our Lives
A Lesson to Sam
Protection
The Truth of Being
Wisdoms of the Infinite Way

WHAT SLOWS OUR SPIRITUAL PROGRESS?

Joel S. Goldsmith

Acropolis Books, Publisher
Longboat Key, Florida

What Slows Our Spiritual Progress? by Joel S. Goldsmith

© 2016 by Acropolis Books

All rights reserved. This publication may not be reproduced, copied or distributed without the express written permission of Acropolis Books, Inc.

Acropolis Books, Inc.
Longboat Key, Florida
www.acropolisbooks.com

> Except the Lord build the house,
> they labour in vain that build it.
>
> Psalm 127

Illumination dissolves all material ties and binds men together with the golden chains of spiritual understanding; it acknowledges only the leadership of the Christ; it has no ritual or rule but the divine, impersonal universal Love; no other worship than the inner Flame that is ever lit at the shrine of Spirit. This union is the free state of spiritual brotherhood. The only restraint is the discipline of Soul; therefore, we know liberty without license; we are a united universe without physical limits; a divine service to God without ceremony or creed. The illumined walk without fear – by Grace.

From the *The Infinite Way* by Joel S. Goldsmith

WHAT SLOWS OUR SPIRITUAL PROGRESS?

Good Evening,

You know, as I look out here, it just seems to be about a waste of time to talk or think about giving a lecture. I don't see anyone out here that I haven't known for quite awhile. If there're any new ones here they are so mixed up in among you that I can't find them. So why don't we start right off now and let's talk seriously about the Infinite way, about you and about me.

The main thing that disturbs me in my travels around the world, meeting Infinite Way students and talking to them, is the slow progress that they're making. Now, I'm not saying that in any critical sense because I'm probably making slower progress than you are. The only thing is you can't see it in me but I can see it in you; and also, even if you can see it in me, you haven't got the right to tell it to me. But it is a fact that our students are making slow progress, slower than is necessary. It is also true that this work is spreading so far, so wide, so rapidly, that it is necessary for more of our students to catch up and at least to arrive at that place where they can do better healing work and more of it.

Right here you may wonder why I'm stressing this healing work so much. I'm stressing it because the Master who has revealed these principles to me has also said that our function is to heal. Heal the sick, raise the dead, preach the Gospel, open the ears of the deaf and open the eyes of the blind, and not in the sense that he was setting up healing clinics across the Holy Lands or that we are expected to set up healing clinics around the world but that healing is an evidence of our grasp on the principle of life. It testifies as to whether or not we understand these principles. In other words, anyone who learns the principles of, let's say electricity, can hook up electric lights. Those of us who can't hook up electric lights, it is very evident that we do not know the principles of electricity. Those of us who cannot drive automobiles now, must admit we do not know the principles involved in driving an automobile, and so we might as well admit that if we can't heal, we have not yet grasped the principles of spiritual healing. It doesn't mean that we may not be able to pass a written examination and get ninety-five percent. Unfortunately that doesn't indicate that one has grasped the principles. It merely indicates that one has memorized words out of a book, and nowhere does it say that memorizing words out of a book is healing consciousness.

Now, in these years of travel, teaching, I think that I have glimpsed some of the reasons that our progress is so slow, and I would say the major reason is that we have not emptied ourselves of our former concepts of truth, and that we are trying to add to what we already know something that is going to be the Messiah or Savior or healing principle. We believe that we can retain the errors of religious teaching and add to those errors some truth which will work miracles for us, and I am convinced that this is our major stumbling block.

I think that this is the same reason that the message of Jesus Christ was never accepted by the Hebrews of his day, with the exception of those few. They had been well taught in the Hebrew faith, in the Hebrew teachings. They were probably what we would call good Hebrews, religious Hebrews, and by the church standards, they probably were entitled to at least ninety percent. Yet they failed utterly to grasp the meaning of the message of Christ Jesus. And why? Because they did not clear out of themselves the misconceptions which they had been taught in the Hebrew faith. And so just like Peter who, not only after three years with the Master, but more years even than that, was still observing the dietetic laws of the Hebrew faith and unwilling to surrender them, and all of the disciples held on fast to the idea that there must be circumcision before anyone could have this great new teaching. For years and years after the Master it was necessary to become a Hebrew before one could be admitted into the circle of the disciples.

We are making that same mistake today. I don't have to remind you that the Christian Church made this mistake also. It is one of the reasons that the Christian Church in this era has to change its mode and means of operation and some of its teaching. It also accepted the ancient Hebrew teachings and then set up a crucifix and called it Christianity. It won't do. It won't do. And now let us spend our remaining time here this evening bringing to light why it won't do.

To begin with, if you have not come far enough out of orthodoxy, you probably believe that you can pray to God and have God take away your sins or your diseases or your lack or your limitation. You probably still believe that you can go to God and pray for peace on earth, or pray for more understanding between men, and in some way or other God will say, "Yes, yes, I didn't do it for you yesterday, but I'll do it for you today.

I didn't do it for the past generations, but I'll make an exception for you and do something for you which I have never done before." And right there you know that it's impossible. You know now, if you stop to think, in this minute, God can't do anything for this world today that God didn't do yesterday and last year and the generation before this, and a dozen generations before that. God is the same yesterday, today, and forever. God is from everlasting to everlasting. Can you then believe that God will do anything for you or for your relatives or for this world that God has not been doing before this? And if you stop to think of that it will automatically change your way of prayer.

In the same way, if you have not yet come far enough out of orthodoxy, you may still be thinking of God as your servant and believing that you can ask God to do things for you and probably it'll be God's good pleasure to run around doing them. Here and now try to understand the nature of God, and see if you cannot understand why the Master said that he was a servant—not God. He was a servant of God, but he never made God a servant of him.

Try to think how many of your prayers indicated that you had some idea that God was going to do your bidding. Let us assume for a moment that you've come further than that, that you understand some of the metaphysical teachings, but you still find it necessary to tell God what things you have need of. You still find it necessary to speak to God or to expect of God that your will be done. Let us think of God for a moment as the infinite Intelligence that created this universe, including you, and then see if you can still believe that you have enough wisdom to tell that God what things you have need of, or when you will need them, or how soon the demonstration must be made so that it isn't going to be too late. Think, think whether or not your prayers or your treatments have been aimed at influencing God in your behalf, or your patient's behalf, or your student's behalf, or even this world's behalf. Think for a moment whether your prayers or your treatments have had, consciously or unconsciously, the desire to influence God, whether it is to bring peace on earth or protect your nation or the world; but think, have your prayers, or have your treatments, in some way or other, consciously or unconsciously been an attempt to influence God, to bring about an activity of God in your behalf or someone else's; then you'll begin to see why your progress has been slow.

You see, in our work in The Infinite Way, principles have been revealed which in some measure have proven to be ... let's use the word "absolute" in the sense that they do result in harmony, peace, joy, protection, and that the only degree in which they have failed, where they seem to have failed, is in the degree of our inability to work consciously with the principles in accord with the principles. In other words, we have tried to mold these principles according to our will, or at least to our understanding, instead of surrendering our understanding in order to receive the wisdom of God.

Now, we will make no progress in the demonstration of the principles of The Infinite Way if we are praying to God as if expecting God to do something for us, or be our servant, or do our will for us, even when that will is good. We will have to learn, if necessary, to train ourselves to stop praying in any way that will have as its background the idea of urging God, coercing God, driving

God, influencing God to do something that God hasn't been doing for a hundred generations—for God cannot be changed. We will not make progress in this work if we are in any way trying to acquaint God with our needs, if we are in any way trying to inform Deity that we have a pain in the right leg or we're overweight all over. There is no use in trying to tell God that we are sick or what ails us. There is no use of telling God what form of good we wish to experience, whether it is of health, harmony, wholeness, completeness, supply, relationship. There is no use of expecting God to heal the sins of our relatives. God is infinite wisdom. You and I aren't yet. Potentially the mind of God is our mind, and we have all of the wisdom of God, but demonstrably we haven't yet proven it, we haven't yet shown it forth. In other words, God is our intelligence, and if we could be still enough, all of the wisdom of God could eventually flow through us individually. We haven't learned to be that still; therefore the degree of our demonstrated wisdom is not sufficient for us to go to God telling God what I need, what you need, what the government needs, what the world needs.

Again, there are those of our students who have backgrounds which have made them believe in the power of thought. Many metaphysicians have accepted the belief that thought is power, that the power of right thinking is a power, that the wrong thinking is an evil power. Many have accepted the belief that some activity of their own mind can produce the miracle of harmony in their experience. You will not make progress in the message of The Infinite Way while those teachings remain embedded in you either consciously *or* unconsciously. Even if you think they are not there, you had better work with yourself to be sure that they are not lurking within you and that you are not still believing that some power of your thought is going to bless you or the world.

Now, so that you may understand this correctly, it is true that on the purely human level of life that your mind can be made a power. It can never be made God-power. Don't ever believe for a minute that your mind can be made God-power—that would be carrying egotism to its ultimate. But to an extent, you can make a power of your mind; you can take your mind and use it as an instrument for accomplishing certain things in this world. But when you do, first of all, don't confuse it with spiritual power because the activity of the human mind has no more relationship to spiritual power than, well, darkness has relationship to light. The power of the human mind is purely human, and has no relationship whatsoever to the divine.

Now, it would only take one minute made up of sixty seconds to prove this to you so that you never again will believe that mind has any relationship to God. Mind has the capacity of both good and evil and God hasn't. That should forever, should forever, show you that mind-action has no relationship whatsoever to God-action, or Spirit-action, or spiritual action. Always remember that the mind of man is capable of good and of evil. Always remember that the mind of man can think good thoughts and bad thoughts, therefore it can have no relationship to God for God is Spirit and there are no pairs of opposites in God; there is no good and evil in God, there is only Spirit.

Try to remember this: When you get into the spiritual realm, you are in an atmosphere where there is neither good nor evil; there is only divine harmony. Two times two are four—that is neither good nor evil, that is just truth. The value of do, re, mi, is do, re, mi, and that's neither good nor evil—that's just do, re, mi. The law of "life begetting life," roses come from rose seeds and you can't get roses from anything but rose seeds. This is neither good nor evil. This is just a fact. This is just being. But when you or I begin to use thought, we can use thought for good or evil. We can use thought to bless, if so be that is our nature, but if we have an opposite kind of a nature, we can use it to curse, and most people are so constituted that they are always at the level where they can use it both ways, and they use it in the good ways for their friends and relatives and, if they can, they'll use it in very bad ways for their enemies. It is for this reason that the Master cautioned against hating your enemies. Why did he caution? Because you have the power to hate—as good as you think you are. You have the power to hate; you have the power to pray for your enemies to be wiped out, to be avenged … for you to be avenged, and your enemies to be destroyed. In other words, as human beings, regardless of how good you are, you're made up of both good and evil, and your thoughts are both good and evil, and they always will be as long as you consciously think through the word "I."

You never will get beyond being good and evil until you go beyond the use of the word "I" and become a clear transparency that does not use the word "I," but lets the Spirit of God flow. Then you have neither friends nor foes because when you are not thinking through your own mind all you are aware of is God and the children of God, and when you see those do evil, whether they are friend or foe, you have only the feeling of compassion: "Foolish people! Foolish people!

Know ye not you're the temple of the living God. You're just postponing the day of your awakening." But there is neither judgment in you, nor criticism, nor condemnation, nor would you, if you had the power, wish them evil, wish them to be punished. Under no circumstances would you wish them to be punished if so be the Spirit of God were flowing. But of your own sake, you believe it right that the man who robs you go to jail, the ones who wronged you be punished, and the citizens of the other countries who have wronged the Star Spangled Banner should all be wiped out with bombs; only don't let it come nigh our dwelling place for we are virtuous.

Always remember that the action of the human mind is composed of both good and evil and therefore it cannot be God; and therefore, if you do heal with the power of your mind, if you do succeed with the power of your mind, acknowledge that it's your mind. Don't ever fool yourself into believing that you have found God-power, for you will only find God-power when you go beyond the use of the mind and let your mind be a servant of God; let God express the thoughts that are to flow into your mind and out through your mind. God says, "*My thoughts are not your thoughts, and My ways are not your ways,*" therefore, the only way that God's thoughts can flow through you is to let yourself be free of thought, be free of mind action and let your mind be the instrument or transparency through which God's thoughts may flow.

This idea was brought out last night in this idea of if you were a composer, if you were an artist, that you would not think—you would get still and listen and be receptive, and you would receive God's thoughts, God's inspiration, God's power. So it is. If you were called to the truth field and you try to sit down and make up messages of truth, you'd soon be in trouble. If you started to remember truth that somebody else wrote, you'd still be in trouble. If you started to invent truth or create it, you'd be worse off. There is only one way that you could really be in the work of truth and that is to arrive at that place where you don't memorize, where you don't think up truth, where you don't try to invent, but where you acknowledge, "*Father, I can of my own self do nothing. If I bear witness to myself, I bear witness to a lie. My doctrine is not mine, but His that sent me,*" and then prove it by being still. Then what comes in, you would verily say, "Oh my heavens! Is that true? I never knew that before this minute," and you would find that it is so.

And in the same way, if you wanted to compose, what's the use of thinking about the music of the masters? That wouldn't be composing. That would be copying, imitating, stealing, borrowing. But to truly compose would be to free one's thoughts of all the melodies one had ever heard, try in so far as possible to forget them, wipe them out, because there are more melodies in God than have ever been heard on earth.

[Music started playing in the background]. I've always wanted to talk with background music. Well, well, well, now we will see if I qualify for vaudeville or moving pictures. [Laughter]

Now, you see, we sit down and read these Infinite Way books, but we must know this: that the books aren't God, and the words in the books aren't God, so we're not going to get our healing from the books or from the type or the particular sequence in which the words are strung together. And so we open our books to read for inspiration and for principles, but then, then the main function begins. Then we close the book and close our eyes. The reading of the books, the unfoldment of these principles, should have brought about an inner stillness, and now the mind should be still so that My words, the words of God, or My peace, the peace of Christ, can descend upon you—not the peace that the world can give you but My peace. And My peace cannot come to a mind that is busy, a mind that is active, a mind that is thinking thoughts that are already in this world. We have shown forth this principle in the subject of supply.

No amount of money or property or security that we could get from each other or from our friends or relatives would be a demonstration of supply. That would be more or less like hanging peaches on an empty peach tree and then taking a photograph of it and saying, "Look how rich my tree is. It's full of peaches." No, no. No, that's not supply. A peach tree, to be rich, has to have its own peaches that have grown and come through all the way up from the roots, all the way from the ground up through the roots and out into the branches and finally dangled off there from these branches, and then you can say, "How rich my tree is."

So with us—supply has to be … not something that we get from each other. It has to be something that unfolds from within our own consciousness. Now that can't happen unless we start with a principle, and a principle can't be anything that would add supply to us, Therefore it rules out praying to God to give us supply, because that would be like one tree praying to another or even up to the sky to have peaches hung on it.

No, we have to start with a principle: *Son, thou art ever with me, and all that I have is thine. The kingdom of God is within me.* God's grace is within me. God's grace functions as my individual life. *All that the Father hath is mine. The earth is the Lord's and the fullness thereof, and all that the Father hath is mine for I and the Father are one. I and the Father are one, and all that the Father hath is mine.* And now attention is centered, not on drawing supply in, not praying for it, not telling God what we need, but sitting quietly in the assurance, *I and the Father are one,* and *all the Father hath is mine.* And then being still; then being still until an answering response comes from within: a stillness, a peace, a joy, sometimes even a voice that says, *"I will never leave thee nor forsake thee.*" Ah! Now then supply begins to unfold from within. It's true that in our picture it may still seem to come from our business, our art, our profession, but the point is that we haven't gone out there to get it. We have acknowledged it as unfolding from within. "Truth is within ourselves," and "we must open out a way for the Imprisoned Splendor to escape."

All right. That word "truth" covers supply, but it also covers the supply of health, home, companionship, harmonious relationship. Therefore, whatever it is that is to bless my life has to flow out from within me. Do you see now how foolish it is then to pray up to God, or even to tell God what you need, because it isn't up there. It's already established within you, and you don't have to tell anyone outside or inside about it, because the all-knowing wisdom of this world already knows and it is Its good pleasure to give. Therefore the attitude in The Infinite Way is to recognize truth is within myself—the truth of supply, the truth of health, the truth of relationship, the truth of joy, the truth of home, the truth of whatever it may be. Therefore I do not look outside my own being; I do not pray for it; I do not treat for it. I rest in this assurance: *The kingdom of God is within me. The earth is the Lord's and the fullness thereof.* And *all that the Father hath is mine.* And then I sit and wait until this sense of peace comes, this click—whatever it may be.

Naturally I am not going to make my demonstration in one day. When it happens it'll happen in one day, but it would be unusual for it to happen the first day that I learned how to pray aright, although it will start with that day. And then as we continue in this practice of letting the mind rest, not praying to God, not telling God, not asking God, not expecting of God, but resting in this: *The kingdom of God is within me. He that is within me knoweth my need,* and *it is His good pleasure to give me the kingdom.* I will let it unfold in God's way. I will let it appear in God's way and in God's time. I will let, let, let—not command, not entreat, not advise. I will *let*.

So you see that before we can make progress in The Infinite Way mode of living, let us be sure that we are not trying to live our former religious life. Let us, first of all, give up the Ten Commandments—that's what the Master said—at least give up nine of them. Don't carry those Ten Commandments over into your New Testament, into your new life. The Master said do away with them and live in two, the first one of the Ten and a new one. And let's forget those other Commandments. And you say, "What! I should forget that I mustn't steal and I mustn't commit adultery?"

Yes, why not? The Master said so. The point is that if you could live by those first two, tell me how you could violate those other nine? And you'd find out why he could safely say, "Don't worry about not stealing or not envying or not committing adultery or not committing murder." I've got you all tied up in knots the minute you love God supremely and your neighbor as yourself, you rule out any possibility of evil human conduct. No one truly loves God and his neighbor and can be unjust, unprincipled, untruthful, dishonest—it's an impossibility if you are loving God supremely and your neighbor as yourself.

Ah! But you see that until you consciously do this, you just carry Judaism over into Christianity. You have heard it said of old what you should do to those who despitefully use you, get back at them twice over; but *I* say unto you, you must consciously bring yourself to a place where if you are going to church or temple or synagogue or reading room to pray for your friends, where you must carry in there at least the equal amount of prayers for the enemy. Otherwise you have not thrown off your old religion, and all you're doing is carrying your former hates and revenges into the new church; and all you do is make a market place out of the new church like the old one was.

In the same way, if you carry into this new consciousness, which you call The Infinite Way—if you carry into this consciousness your old mode of prayers and treatment, you are not keeping this consciousness an Infinite Way consciousness, and therefore, you can only demonstrate what you bring in. And so if you divide it up into a little old theology, and a little old mental science, and a little of the spiritual science, well, that's what you bring forth—a little of each, for like begets like.

In this book *The Art of Spiritual Healing*, you have a chapter on "Is God a Servant?" and as you read it, well, I know that there is going to be very few of us that won't have to say, "To some extent that's exactly how I've been praying. That in the back of my mind, that's what I had. 'Now, God, I'm telling you what, but now you do it. I've told you God, now I'll sit here and wait until you perform it.'" And you'll see to what extent you have made a servant of God *in your own mind* because actually, it can't be done.

In this book, there's a chapter, "The Relationship of Oneness." As you study it, see to what extent you still have in mind wanting someone else corrected, someone else improved, someone else healed; and then you will know to what degree you have not accepted Infinite Way principles. Therefore, to that extent you haven't demonstrated

Infinite Way principles, because The Infinite Way is based primarily on one Self and that One, God—that One, therefore, not needing correction, improving, healing, reforming, or enriching. So we find out that as you search yourself in the reading of this, you see to what extent you have violated the principles of the Infinite Way, and then you will know to what extent you have failed and why. I use the word "you" but don't think for a minute that I don't mean myself, because regardless of how far we go on the spiritual path, remember that each one of us, to some extent is carrying over the past, the past of our ancestors, the past of our youthful beliefs.

I think I've told some of our classes of an experience that always reminds me of this, the time when my mother told me there was no Santa Claus, and there was no use of hanging up the stockings, and she took me around to the department stores to prove it to me. Every store had a Santa Claus, and so she said, "You see, there is no Santa Claus; it's just a made-up man." But now you know, my mother didn't convince me at all, and I hung up my stockings anyhow—just in case. No one can convince us that the God of our ancestors doesn't exist. We have to outgrow that ourselves and we have to do it consciously—and it isn't easy. Paul calls it dying daily. And if you don't think it is dying daily, try it. Try to outgrow those early religious teachings, and if you want a task more difficult, try to outgrow your metaphysical teachings. Try to outgrow that belief that thought is power—probably the thought that *your* thought is a good power, and now let's protect ourselves because I know somebody whose thought is bad power. And so you will see then, that you'll agree with me eventually that mind is both good and evil, and it's only that yours and mine is good, but the other fellow's is evil. But you will come to agree eventually that mind-power can be good and mind-power can be evil, and if we want to rise into the Spirit of God we must rise above good and evil and we can't do it while we're in the realm of thought. We can't do it while we're in the realm of mind-power.

No, you've probably seen books on how you can make plants grow with the right thought and how you can destroy them with the bad thought. It's true enough, you can. And that proves my point that mind can't be God.

Never let anyone convince you that God has evil power. There too, you have to wipe out a lot of orthodoxy. Don't ever let anyone tell you that God calls your beloved ones home. When we die or pass on, it is only for one of two reasons. One, no one knew how to keep us alive, and in our ignorance, either material medica let us die or metaphysics let us die, or the time had come for our transition. No one is going to remain on earth forever. If anyone was to have accomplished that, it would have been done by Lao Tze, by Buddha, by Jesus, and by John. Above all people of the world, they would have made that demonstration if it had been intended; and I know really a half a dozen more who would have made it had it been intended that we should remain on this plane of existence forever. There comes a time when, just as we leave childhood for maturity, so we must leave maturity for something even beyond that. In the same way that there is a time in human history when people leave their animalistic way of living for the Ten Commandments, and learn how to be good human beings. But there also comes a time for outgrowing the Ten Commandments and living as spiritual beings.

And so there comes a time for the transition from this plane of consciousness to another activity, another form of activity, another progressive step. And so we will leave this plane as all others have done, but remember that there are two ways of going: one is through ignorance of how to stay until our time has arrived, and the other is by going when our time is. Now, do not accept the belief that there is a certain age when we must go, because there are children who must go at three, four, five, ten, twelve, fifteen, or twenty years because they have evolved out of whatever was necessary. There will be those going in their twenties and in their thirties, and in their forties, because they have evolved into the next period; and there will be those who will be compelled to remain here until they're eighty or ninety or a hundred because they are not yet evolved into that experience. But never let anyone tell you that God is responsible for death, for *God has no pleasure in your dying; turn ye and live*. Let no one convince you that three score years and ten is a good time to get ready to go, because it may not be your time, although you can make it so by accepting a world belief.

The gist of what I'm saying here tonight is this: we can all make more rapid progress in our spiritual development than we are making, and the biggest barrier there is to that progress is what we are carrying over into our present consciousness from either orthodox beliefs or metaphysical beliefs, and the quickest way to progress is to start eradicating these. You can't eradicate them without first becoming aware that they're there, and this calls for self-examination.

When you read any of the Writings of the The Infinite Way and come to specific principles, stop and ponder them and see if you are not still accepting the opposite of them. If you come to principles of prayer and treatment, stop and ponder and see if you are not still accepting older modes, different modes; see if you have adjusted yourself to these specific principles and above all things—above all things—remember that you are being presented with a principle that is so difficult to accept because it has never been presented in any religious teaching that has appeared on earth. And yet, it is the major principle of our work, and that is: there are not two powers. In the human scene there is good and evil. But that is only because as humans we accept the belief in good and evil. As absolute truth there are not two powers, there is only one.

In proportion as you can bring yourself to that understanding, that awareness, and the ability to stand on that truth in spite of appearances to the contrary, will you demonstrate according to Infinite Way principles. Try to understand that in the Infinite Way you do not use Truth to overcome error. Try to understand that you do not go to God to have God destroy evil. Try to understand that you are never using one power to overcome or destroy another power, that in the Infinite Way you are abiding in the truth that there is one power and all else is the arm of flesh or nothingness. You must bring yourself to a state of consciousness in which you can say—if it is anything discordant, "Oh, that is the devil or carnal mind or mortal mind," meaning I don't have to be concerned about it because it isn't power.

The moment that you believe that you have something for which you need the power of God you are outside the realm of the Infinite Way. The very moment you believe that you're aware of something that needs a truth, you are outside the realm of The Infinite Way. You don't need any truth for anything in the Infinite Way. You don't need any God for anything in The Infinite Way. God is already doing God's work. God is already about God's business. In fact, God was doing it in the beginning before Abraham was, and God will be doing it until the end of time, so just let God be about God's business and be grateful that you don't have to remind his that the tide should come in at 4:12 tomorrow morning. Be grateful that you don't have to remind God that the sun must come up tomorrow morning. Just be grateful that God is about God's business, has been, will be, and you don't have to remind God—not about anything that is going on in this world, but you do have to remind yourself morning, noon, and night that God is about God's business and all is well. God's in His heaven; all's well on earth, and rest, rest in that consciousness.

Made in the USA
Columbia, SC
26 January 2023